Oakland Community College

C0-AWD-650

Farmington Hills, MI 48334

LD 571 .B6733 S34 1988
Schermeister, Phil.
Brigham Young University

occOR Oct-30-1991 22:03

DATE DUE

GAYLORD 234   PRINTED IN U. S. A.

Oakland Community College
Orchard Ridge Campus Library
27055 Orchard Lake Road
Farmington Hills, MI 48334

DEMCO

If men, and we would add women, would be great in goodness, they must be intelligent, for no man can do good unless he knows how; therefore seek after knowledge, all knowledge, and especially that which is from above, which is wisdom to direct in all things, and if you find anything that God does not know, you need not learn that thing; but strive to know what God knows, and use that knowledge as God uses it, and then you will be like him; you will ... have charity, love one another, and do each other good continually, and forever...

Brigham Young, Heber C. Kimball, and Willard Richards

Brigham Young Statue with "Y" Mountain

BRIGHAM YOUNG
UNIVERSITY

PHOTOGRAPHED BY PHIL SCHERMEISTER

HARMONY HOUSE
PUBLISHERS LOUISVILLE

LD
571
.B6733
S34
1988
OR 11/91

Beehive atop Karl G. Maeser Building

Executive Editors: William Butler and William Strode
Library of Congress Catalog Number: 87-083164
Hardcover International Standard Book Number 0-916509-40-0
Printed in USA by Pinaire Lithographing Corp., Louisville, Kentucky
First Edition printed Fall, 1988 by Harmony House Publishers,
P.O. Box 90, Prospect, Kentucky 40059 (502)228-2010 / 228-4446
Copyright © 1988 by Harmony House Publishers
Photographs Copyright © 1988 by Phil Schermeister

This book or portions thereof may not be reproduced in any form without
permission of Harmony House Publishers. Photographs may not be
reproduced in any form without permission of Phil Schermeister.

Old "Y" Victory Bell

Karl G. Maeser Building

Previous page: Provo Temple

BYU Traditions: A Legacy Worth Continuing

To each of us, Brigham Young University is different. No single volume can hope to capture all of our past memories and experiences. Yet this volume attempts to show how the total of our collective impressions fits into a beautiful montage that comes together to suggest an ever-growing whole.

A great university is not just students, even though they become the one single eternal element. Here they learn how to give, how to share, how to serve...

Who would ever have thought in 1876 that George Sutherland, an unknown little boy from Provo and member of one of the first classes at BYU, would go on to become a justice of the U.S. Supreme Court?

Or that Sheila Olsen '60 of Idaho Falls could endure her immobilizing physical handicaps and still cheerfully raise a large, outstanding family and support her husband as a politically active state party chairman and lawyer? And even after his death, continue to teach and inspire family and community members.

Or that Bill Allen '68 of Atlanta would be so dedicated as to interrupt his professional career, taking leave of absence for an entire year, in order to head up the state program for the Georgia Special Olympics?

A great university captures the spark of lofty purpose that is in us all and fans that spark into a blazing, consuming fire — all this with the help of great teachers who, sometimes not so gently, blew on the flame...

A Wayne B. Hales, beloved gentleman and a champion of science, opening the shutter of the mind and exposing it to physics, astronomy, mathematics, and all related disciplines for eager minds to grasp and then to go on to exciting new discoveries of their own.

A Harold R. Clark, terror to the unprepared in the business classroom — yet a man of great culture and personal warmth. Always seen striding rapidly across the campus and yet never too busy to wave and shout a greeting across the campus to a lost and lonely freshman.

A great university is not just a collection of beautiful buildings that hosted the activities of learning; a great university becomes a collection of hallowed halls that stores our memories until we can one day return...

The old Maeser Building, now restored to its pristine beauty after a lifetime of multi-uses as lecture halls, presidents' offices, registration office, archives, hospital, or of course, as a favorite proposal place. This grand old edifice lives on still in grace and beauty.

Knight Hall with its old-world atmosphere, evoking memories of dormitory escapades, of friendships, of romance, and even of romances broken. Collective centuries of "midnight hours" spent there in studying for that next big exam.

The science labs with their flashes, rumbles, and little frogs that gave their all that we might learn; the art rooms with their north-facing windows pulling out our attention to spectacular peaks beyond.

The main staircase in the library with its green steps, now beginning to show the wear of so may as they trudged up or down to search for that one more article or chart. To step down those polished steps is to feel the millions of others who have gone down them before to drink from a mighty well of knowledge. To step up is to be satisfied that the process will still come for countless others.

Yes, this university is a beautiful and sacred place, made so by the legacy left and a vision yet to come.

Caroline Hemenway Harman Conference Center

VISION AND SACRIFICE
The Foundations of Brigham Young University

On October 16, 1875, Brigham Young deeded 2.1 acres of land at Third West and Center Street in Provo, Utah, to Abraham O. Smoot and six other trustees for the establishment of the Brigham Young Academy. President Young specified in his deed of trust that "all pupils shall be instructed in reading, penmanship, orthography, grammar, geography, and mathematics, together with such other branches as are usually taught in an academy of learning; and the Old and New Testaments, the Book of Mormon, and the Book of Doctrine and Covenants shall be read and their doctrines inculcated in the academy." As the institution has grown from an obscure elementary school to a prominent Amerian university many people have worked together to keep Brigham Young's trust to develop a uniquely spiritual academic center.

In April of 1876, after the academy operated four months with a temporary principal, President Brigham Young called Karl G. Maeser, a talented German schoolmaster, into his office and asked him to become the first permanent principal of Brigham Young Academy. Maeser accepted the calling, together with Brigham Young's charge to teach even the multiplication tables with the spirit of God. The term began on April 24, 1876, with twenty-nine students. None of the students progressed beyond the fourth grade that first year, but Maeser organized some of the more talented pupils into a teacher training class.

On January 27, 1884, the Lewis Building, home of the academy, burned to the ground, and the school entered a decade of crisis. While the academy moved its facilities to the ZCMI warehouse at Fifth South and what is now University Avenue, the Board of Trustees purchased the block at Fifth North and University. By winter of 1884, the new Academy Building's foundation was in place, but financial problems forced the school to postpone its completion until 1891. Depending solely on tuition and private contributions for support, the academy almost collapsed during the recession of the late 1880's, but Abraham Smoot (who had had to leave a comfortable home in Salt Lake to accept a call as stake president in Provo) and other members of the Board of Trustees personally subsidized its operation.

Family Statue

On January 4, 1892, the Academy Building was dedicated, and Principal Maeser, having recruited a component faculty in spite of the financial difficulties, retired to devote full-time to his calling as superintendent of Church schools. His replacement, Benjamin Cluff, Jr., dedicated himself to expanding the work of the school to include college degrees. Accordingly, in 1895, his title was changed from principal to president. BYA continued its financial struggles, and many feared it was doomed when President Abraham O. Smoot died in 1895 (deep in debt for endorsing loans made to the academy), but in 1896 the LDS Church assumed the school's debts and incorporated the Brigham Young Academy as a subsidiary of the Church.

The Academy continued to upgrade its Collegiate Department until, in acknowledgement of the achievement, the name of the school was changed to Brigham Young University on October 23, 1903.

In April, 1904, George H. Brimhall, himself trained as a teacher at the academy, became the school's fourth president. Brimhall worked to increase BYU's preeminence as a teacher training institution and to improve its overall collegiate program. In 1906 the Bachelor of Arts degree replaced the Bachelor of Pedagogy degree, and ten years later the Board of Trustees authorized a Master of Arts program.

In 1909 work began on the Maeser Memorial, the first university building on Temple Hill. As the building neared completion in 1912, BYU,

desperate for money again, planned to sell its remaining property on the hill. Instead of the graduation speaker's planned sales pitch to the community, however, he told of a vision he'd seen of thousands of young students emerging full of faith from countless "temples of learning" covering the hill. In response, Jesse Knight stood and shouted "We won't sell an acre!" and donated money on the spot, with many more contributors following. The university was saved by those people's faith in the promise of future generations.

President Franklin S. Harris, an internationally recognized agronomist, began his tenure in 1921. The administration and faculty worked vigorously during this time to transform BYU into an accredited university, even organizing a graduate division. In 1923 the school adopted the cougar as its official mascot (and raised tuition from $23 to $38 per quarter)! A symbol of the school's growing academic stature was the Heber J. Grant Library, dedicated in 1925. Throughout the years the library became well stocked, largely through the efforts of Alice Louise Reynolds, one of BYU's most enduringly popular teachers. In 1928 BYU was finally accredited by the Association of American Universities.

While most Ameican universities suffered from declining enrollment during the Depression, BYU enjoyed a steady increase in student enrollment and academic prominence. In 1940 the Division of Religion was organized, giving formal structure to a program of theological classes that had been an important part of the university from the beginning. Also in the 1940's, the Joseph Smith Building was dedicated; it became a center for BYU student activities and commencement exercises.

When Howard S. McDonald, superintendent of Salt Lake City public schools, was appointed president in 1945, the school faced the challenge of handling an enrollment that increased as rapidly after World War II as it had decreased earlier. (In 1943 enrollment fell to a low of 884, with women outnumbering men six to one; in 1946 it was back up to 4,366, many of whom were veterans.) BYU responded to the challenge of skyrocketing enrollment by increasing student housing, planning for the expansion of academic facilities, and creating a comprehensive program for the counseling, housing, feeding, and health care of students.

In 1951 Ernest L. Wilkinson, a prominent graduate of BYU who was practicing law in Washington, D.C., replaced the acting president to become the seventh president of the university. The next two decades saw the largest program for recruiting students and increasing physical facilities in the history of the school. Starting from a physical plant that included only the Maeser Memorial, the Grant Library, the Brimhall Building, the Eyring Science Center, and the Joseph Smith Building on upper campus, BYU underwent construction of scores of academic buildings and a large system of student housing. By 1959 the student body had grown to 13,326. Church programs kept pace with the growing student body, and the first campus stake of the LDS Church was organized at the school in 1956. Anxious that academic progress match the school's physical growth, Wilkinson received authority to establish the university's first doctoral program in 1957.

In 1971, Dallin H. Oaks, a graduate of BYU and a professor of law at the University of Chicago, took the helm. With a near-capacity enrollment of 26,000, the next nine years were "a period of maturing, deepening, and refining." They saw the establishment of the J. Reuben Clark Law School, the year-round academic calendar, the General Education Program, the Ezra Taft Benson Agriculture and Food Institute,

the Institute of Professional Accountancy, the School of Management and more. This was a time for the university to come of age, to be recognized as a top undergraduate institution. These were also the years when BYU standards were most threatened by U.S. government regulations, when Brigham Young University emerged as the leader of American private colleges and universities in their legal struggle for independence. Then-commissioner of the Church Educational System Jeffrey R. Holland described BYU at this time as "prepared to take [its] place in the world."

Dr. Holland was appointed in 1980 to be the ninth president of BYU, after a 20-year association with the university as commissioner, dean, and professor. An undeviating commitment to the highest standards of achievement characterizes his tenure: "Excellence must be our hallmark here, from the arts to zoology, for both students and faculty." During the 80's, the university has seen major departmental reorganizations and constructed the two largest buildings in its history to accommodate an enrollment of around 27,000. 1982 inaugurated the "Excellence in the Eighties" campaign, which raised over $100 million to strengthen the school's infrastructure — buildings, equipment, etc. — while a later fund-raising effort concentrated on increasing available money for endowed chairs and scholarships. And the exposure accompanying the 1984 NCAA football championship has also helped to make the nation aware both of BYU's tremendous athletic programs and of its standards and ideals; since then the university has continued to grow in stature and reputation.

Brigham Young University has seen remarkable changes throughout its history. Constant amid the change, however, have been the remarkable contributions the school has received from dedicated men and women and the commitment of its students, faculty, and alumni to ideals like virtue and truth. "Ideals are like stars: you choose them as your guides, and following them you will reach your destiny." As these traditions continue, BYU will reach its destiny, and become, in the words of President Spencer W. Kimball, "an educational Mt. Everest."

Karl G. Maeser Statue

Previous page: Corey Lecture Hall

Who are we then, here at BYU? And what does God expect us to do? For one thing, he expects us to remember we are heirs of a gospel dispensation that had among its earliest commandments the challenge to seek ... diligently and teach one another words of wisdom; yea, to seek ... out of the best books ... learning, even by study and also by faith.

Jeffrey R. Holland

Deseret Towers Dorm and Carillon Bell Tower

The uniqueness of Brigham Young University lies in its special role, education for eternity, which it must carry in addition to the usual tasks of a university. This means concern – curricular and behavioral – for not only the whole man, but for the eternal man. Where all universities seek to preserve the heritage of knowledge that history has washed to their feet, this faculty has a double heritage – the preserving the knowledge of men and the revealed truths sent from heaven.

President Dallin H. Oaks

Caroline Hemenway Harman Building

The Tree of Wisdom

Spencer W. Kimball Tower

N. Eldon Tanner Building

I believe that you who have been trained in the Brigham Young University have a unique philosophy of life. You should have had already inculcated into your minds, hearts, and souls, in addition to a broad knowledge of the latest trends of thought, an understanding of and an appreciation for many of the eternal verities of life – that priceless heritage of youth which transcends in abiding value the ordinary concepts that constitute the teachings generally disseminated. We should have our feet here planted firmly on the rock of ages.

Judge David J. Wilson, Baccalaureate service, May 30, 1963

A good tree cannot bring forth evil fruit – and a city on a hill cannot be hid. If our lives are structured according to the law of God – if we see His Presence burning in every bush, on every mountainside – if, wherever we are, we can say, "This is the place where I am called to serve"– then men will be drawn toward what we stand for, as they were drawn to follow Moses and Brigham Young and other leaders whose lives embodied the eternal principles.

Cecil B. DeMille
Commencement, May 31, 1957

Aspen Grove, Rock Canyon

"Y" Mountain

Harold B. Lee Library

Education is the power to think clearly, to act well in the world's work, and to appreciate life.

Brigham Young

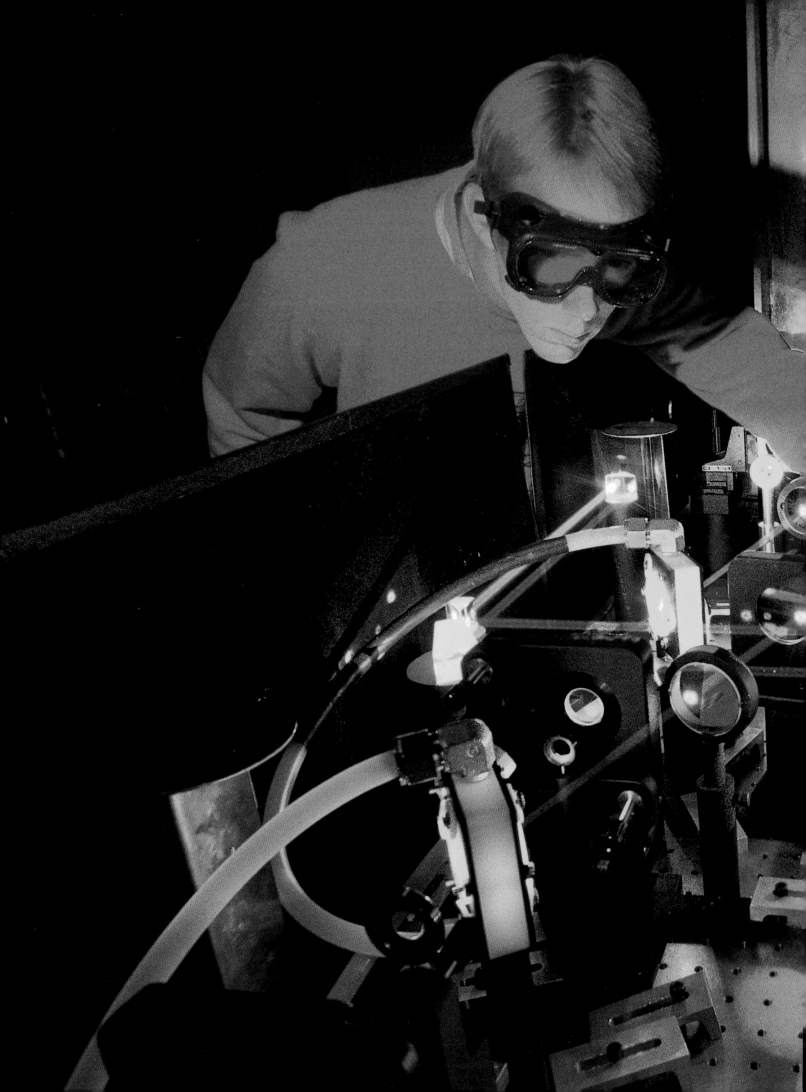

N. Eldon Tanner Building

Karl G. Maeser Building stairway

Lover's Lane

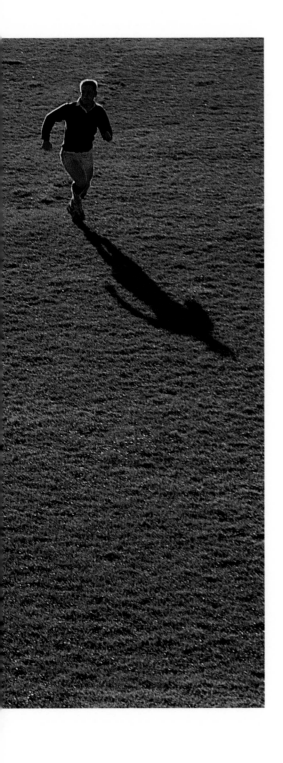

Marriott Center devotional

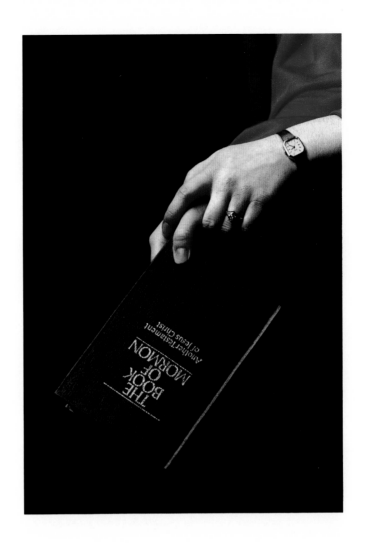

Tower, lower campus

Missionary Training Center

True education does not consist merely in the acquiring of a few facts of science, history, literature, or art, but in the development of character.

David O. McKay

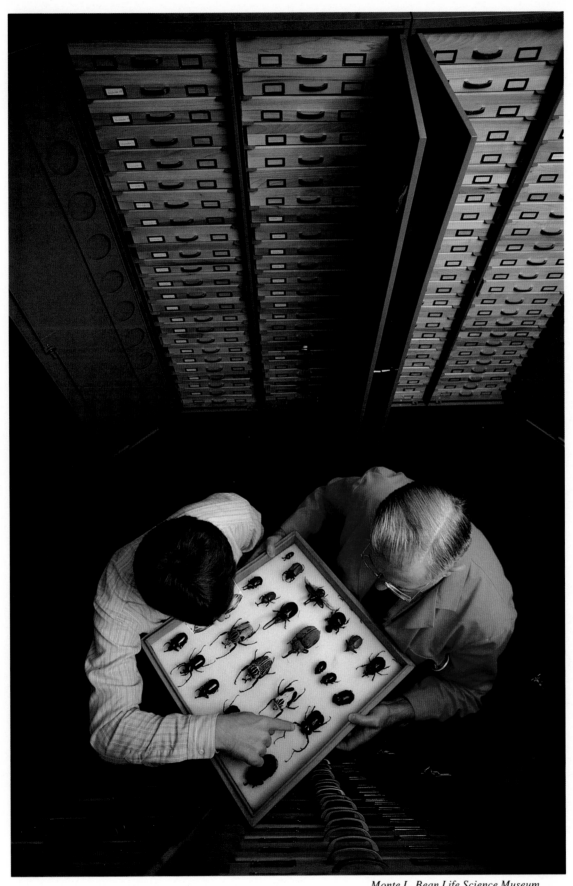

Monte L. Bean Life Science Museum

ROTC

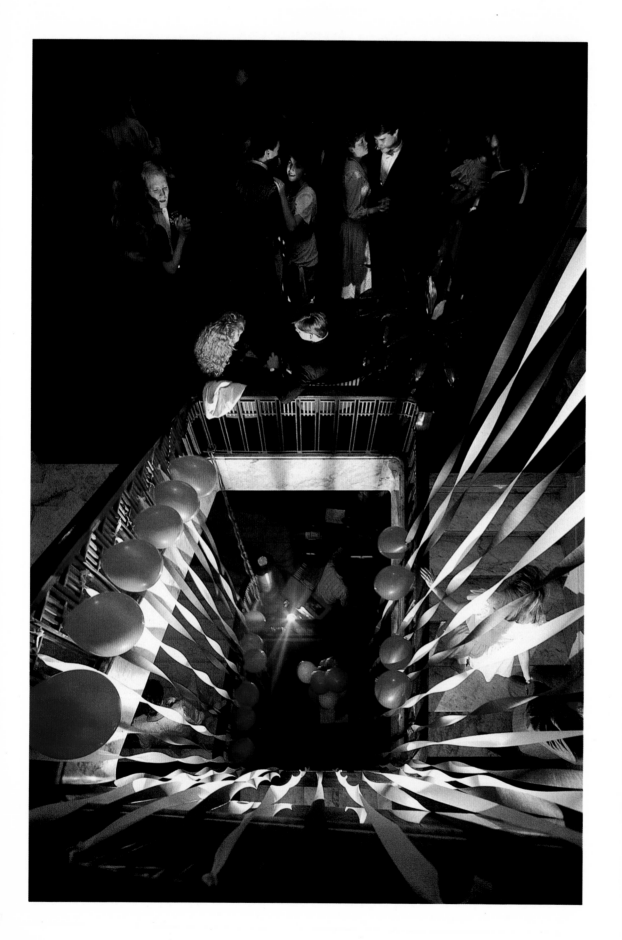

Homecoming Bon Fire

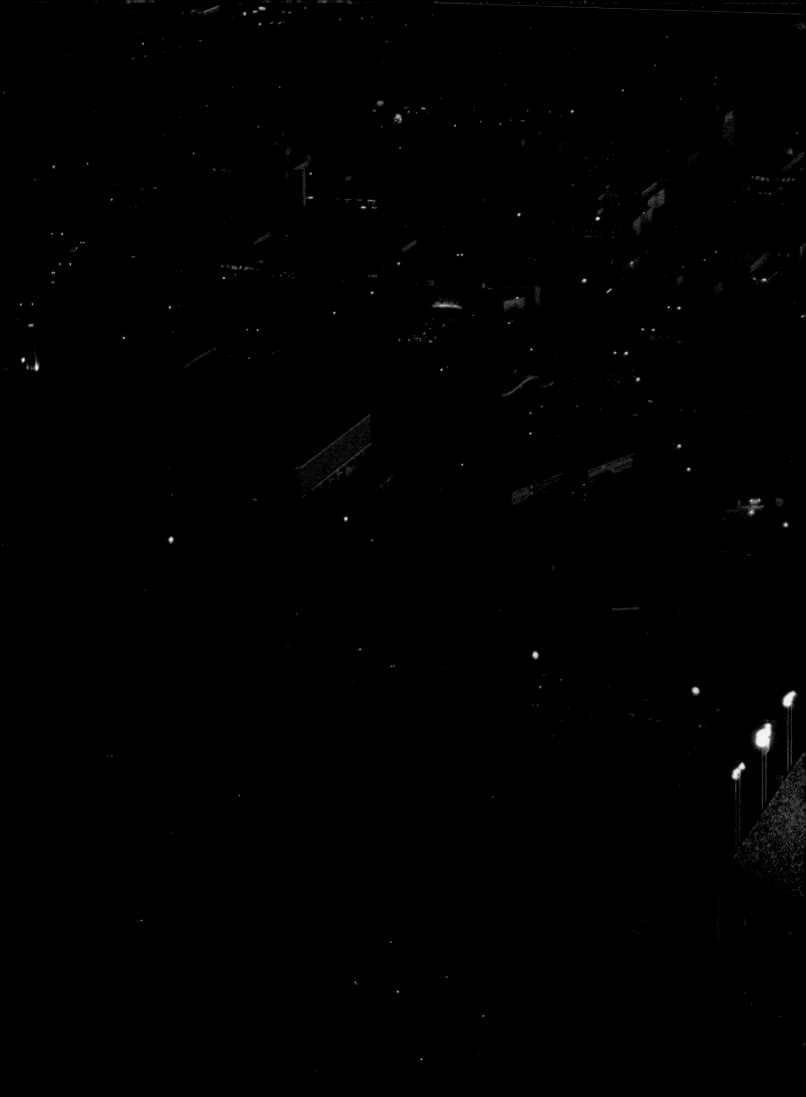

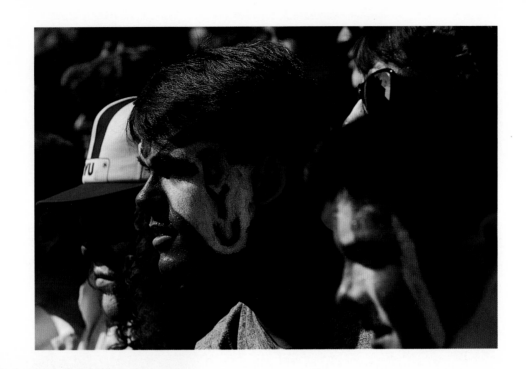

Alumni Reunion Banquet

George Albert Smith Fieldhouse

J. Willard Marriott Center

Franklin S. Harris Fine Arts Center

BYU is sometimes perceived as being a polyester, middle-of-the-road, football-oriented, Republican, heavy cholesterol breakfast sort of place. And that really disguises the fact that I think we have one of the most international campuses in the country. My particular research emphasis right now is on tropical ecology and ethnobotany, and my colleagues are amazed that I have undergraduates working for me who can speak everything from Quechua Indian languages to Tongan.

Paul A. Cox, Associate Professor of Botany and Science, in *BYU Today*, April, 1987

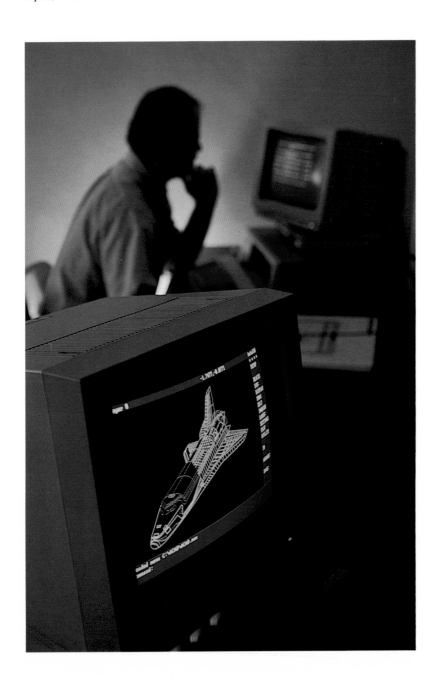

Planetarium, Carl F. Eyring Physical Science Center

Previous page: Testing Center, Heber J. Grant Building

Karl G. Maeser Building

I believe it is reasonable and proper to say that those who have made possible your education here at Brigham Young University have a right to and will expect that you will accomplish more with the education that you will have received here than if you had earned comparable degrees from other great institutions of higher learning. In too many other universities, they have created for themselves what may be properly described as a total subjective world; for it is a world in which no value judgments are encouraged or permitted. Authority is not accepted – there is little to distinguish one individual from another. Here, you have had the advantage of an institution that adheres to basic principles, not only in education, but in the matter of living itself. At this university, there is recognition that the institution's primary duty is to provide every student with the skills needed for responsible citizenship.

Joseph Rosenblatt, Commencement Address, April 21, 1978

Let the morality of the Graduates of this University provide the Music of hope for the inhabitants of this planet.

Spencer W. Kimball

This nation has been involved in monumental discussions and far-reaching political activities that all relate closely to a principle that all of you at this great university know so well. The six words in the motto of Brigham Young University make a profound statement: The glory of God is intelligence.

T. H. Bell, U.S. Secretary of Education, Commencement, April 20, 1984

I have had a dream – I have seen Temple Hill, present site of the campus, filled with buildings – great temples of learning and I have decided to remain and do my part in contributing to the fulfillment of that dream.

Karl Gottfried Maeser

LOOKING BACK AT

BRIGHAM YOUNG
UNIVERSITY

(Above) Brigham Young, second President of The Church of Jesus Christ of Latter-day Saints and the founder of the University that bears his name. This photograph is believed to be from the year 1871.

The Lewis Building (right) was the first home of the Brigham Young Academy, having been purchased by Brigham Young from brick manufacturer Jesse William Lewis. After seven years of crowded occupancy by the Academy, President Smoot added 3 rooms to the structure; in 1883, two more rooms were added. Fire destroyed the Lewis Building in 1884.

When Principal Maeser opened the school in 1876 he was faced with inadequate facilities and poorly prepared students. However, Maeser turned the school around, demanding discipline and courtesy. He came to be revered by his students, some of whom are shown here in 1885.

After the Lewis Building burned in 1884, the Academy moved into this building, the ZCMI warehouse. Classes opened on September 1, 1884 and remained here for eight years. Here the students assemble for a photograph.

Room D of the Academy Building, used here in 1905 as a study room, was the site of assemblies until College Hall was built in 1898.

Probably the finest school building in Utah at that time, the new Academy Building was one of the largest of its kind in the Rocky Mountain region. The first Founder's Day celebration is shown here in 1900.

The Provo City Railway Company was built in 1889 and ran until 1896 on University Avenue and on Center Street to the Provo Resort at Utah Lake. "Puffing Billy," the small steam engine, saw busy service during summers as residents headed for the beach.

The Class of 1896, as photographed in 1893, in front of the Academy Building shortly after its completion.

Built by the Saints of Utah Valley over a 15 year period ending in 1898, the Provo Tabernacle was the site of many BYU commencement exercises and music recitals. Some of the artists who played here include Sergei Rachmaninoff, Paul Robeson, and the Metropolitan Quartet.

This turn-of-the-century photograph shows how the College Building, at right, was joined to the Academy Building, on the left, in 1898.

The Missionary and Preparatory Building was home for the Missionary Department and the many missionaries who travelled the world in service to the Church.

Challenged by the juniors' "1907" painted on the mountainside, the seniors of that year decided to one-up by painting the University symbol. All 3 letters— B-Y-U— were originally planned but upkeep of one was tedious enough. Every year on Y Day, thousands of students revitalized it up with stones, cement and white-wash, some of which is being stirred by students at left.

The campus in 1902 included: the Training School Building; the College Building; and the High School Building

A very special occasion in Provo, September 24, 1909 — U.S. President William H. Taft visited and toured the new Brigham Young Campus. This crowd awaited his arrival at the train station.

In 1917, as war spread throughout Europe, President Brimhall suggested making Brigham Young an official camp of the Student Army Training Corps. His proposal was later approved by President Joseph F. Smith. This photograph, taken in 1918, shows SATC soldiers standing on the steps of the Maeser Building.

Stadium construction in 1927 included grading the earth with horse and mule teams.

The football field and stadium were constructed on the west side of Temple Hill and completed in 1928. Here, concrete is being poured for the seats.

The Brigham Young campus in 1929. On Temple Hill were the Maeser Memorial Building (foreground); the Mechanic Arts Building, a one-story structure; and the Grant Library (right).

Track and field was a particularly popular sport among Brigham Young students in the 20's and 30's. The University hosted one of the largest track and field meets in the country in these years.

Many early football games were played at Timp Park with automobiles and fans lining the sidelines. Later, football games were moved to the old grandstands on the Upper Campus, which until then had only been used for track.

The George Albert Smith Fieldhouse was home for capacity crowds of 11,000 BYU basketball fans from 1951 to 1971.

The University's intercollegiate basketball games were played in the Women's Gymnasium from 1912 until the George Albert Smith Fieldhouse was built in 1951. This game was against the University of Utah in 1937.

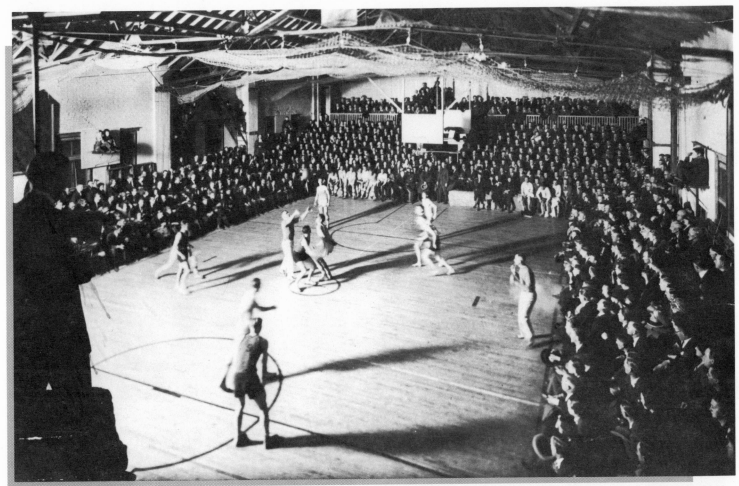

The old Men's Gym was the site of BYU basketball games until the move was made to the Women's Gymnasium in 1912. Notice in this photograph, circa 1910, the spectators perched on the side baskets and the referee's center toss to start the game.

The Joseph Smith Memorial Building now stands where the running track and playing field used to be in 1904. The grandstand (right) was destroyed by fire in April, 1932. A favorite picnicking site for Provoans was the Raymond Grove (left), named after Raymond Wright.

Semi-Centennial celebrations at the Maeser Building, 1925.

The Heber J. Grant Library was dedicated in October, 1925, replacing the old library in the Education Building. It was the first building on campus dedicated solely to a library since 1875. It served the University as the library until 1959, when expanding enrollment brought about the construction of the new library.

Students in a study room of the Education Building, 1925.

President Harry S. Truman (center), with Brigham Young University President Ernest L. Wilkinson (left) and Church President David O. McKay (right), October 6, 1952, before President Truman's address to a special assembly of students in the old stadium.

The fear of God is the beginning of all wisdom.
This life is one great assignment, and that is to become
absorbed with the principles of immortality and eternal life.
Man grows only with his higher goals.
Never let anything impure enter here.

Karl G. Maeser, in a final message to students two months
before his death in 1901.